The Life of a Borderline Personality: A Close Look Into The Mind Of A Borderline Personality

(Mental Health Series 1)

By Nicole Lev

STOP: READ THIS FIRST

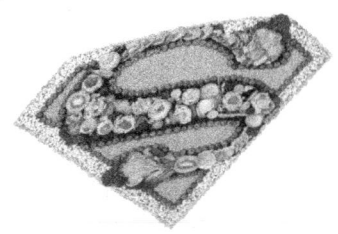

SUPER FRUITS and VEGGIES

20 Superfoods That Will Transform Your Health

Hanna M. Krem

Just to say thank you for downloading my book, I would like to give you my 20 Super Fruits And Veggies Report That My Friend Wrote 100% FREE! This guide has helped me immensely. By eating the better foods, my mind started functioning better

DOWNLOAD NOW

(Or go to http://www.strengthrecipe.com/free)

TABLE OF CONTENTS

The Mind

I don't really know how I got here or what force in this universe brought me into this chaos that I call "my life". All I know is that adaptation is key. If you are able to emotionally adapt in any situation than you will survive this brutal world. However, sometimes the darkness still manages to win over and you can feel yourself slipping from the person that you are into the person that only appears in your nightmares. This person doesn't smile; perhaps, he doesn't know how to smile. Perhaps he knows something you don't know. He knows your most uncontrollable fears and he smiles at them. He finds you pathetic and irrelevant. All you can do is fight him. Fight for that person you know you are, the person who always sees the light. Fight for that child who never pitied himself. Fight for the mother who did the best she could out of all she had. Never forget where you came from because if you're still here, maybe it's fate.

But what do you do if you are not able to adapt? You lose yourself.

Everyday is a struggle. It's a never-ending emotional roller coaster of wants and needs. Do I know what I actually want or need? I have no idea to this day. I lost a part of me a long time ago. That girl that I still freshly remember in my head is somewhere inside of me but she doesn't come out for long. She's a glimpse of who I am, or possibly of who I was. The person who gets to see this girl is lucky. He'll hold on to me just to see a glimpse of her again but then, after a period of time, he realizes that I'm not her anymore. This angers him and he usually runs. I warned him though. I told him I have demons that feed on her very existence. Maybe that's what it is. Demons.

Growing up

I grew up with both my parents. Happily married, I always tell people. But isn't that a sweet lie. My father was a belligerent drunk around the time I was 10 years old. He always knew how to swig a whole bottle down and trip over himself on the way home. Sometimes, he would come home in states where he couldn't hold his own weight up. My mother would help him walk to the bedroom, make the bed, and put him to sleep. She couldn't stand to sleep with him so she would sleep in my bed for a long time. Every night she would go out for a cigarette, cry a bit here and there, and then she would crawl into my bed and try to doze off. Now that I think about it, she probably stayed up for hours before she could fall asleep. But I didn't know that, I was still a child. I don't blame my father for anything because after growing up I know now that he drinks for reasons. He drank when he couldn't make any money. He, just like me, was slipping into somebody else. Maybe that's why I think he and I are very alike. We both know what it's like to not be ourselves most of the time.

Everyday is a struggle when you live with borderline personality disorder. Waking up is one of the biggest struggles because the mood you wake up in is the prime determinant of how the rest of your day is going to go. Additionally, even if your day is going fantastically, it could all change in an instant? You might take a step back and ask yourself why you snapped and you can't even find a logical explanation because this rage just exploded from the deepest parts of you. You're like a kettle that can boil over any second. Everyday is a surprise for you and to others. Relationships are the worst. It's impossible to have a healthy relationship with a person who won't be able to completely understand your disorder. Anything can set you off into a spiral of paranoia, instability, and a surge of unacceptable emotions. You might say that it's controllable. However, it's like a disease that eats you alive. You can't control your own paranoid thoughts. You keep visualizing the worst situation happening. You might feel abandoned or just really hurt. You're becoming impulsive and all you can think about is picking up that knife and slitting your arm. You want to jump off the balcony and just end it there. Maybe everybody will feel bad after and cry at your funeral you think. This is when survival isn't a concern anymore. You just want the pain to end.

I think the pain I get in my chest from all the anxiety is the worst feeling I've ever felt. It's like somebody just sat right on top of your chest and all the wind got knocked out of you. I fear that this pain is endless. I fear my child feels this pain. Maybe he'll come out exactly like me. That'll be my biggest regret. The idea that I made this innocent child suffer is the worst possible outcome. I won't stand myself in that moment.

Married

My husband is a good man. He is literally, one in a million. I didn't have too many experiences with men but enough bad experiences to know what I was looking for by the time I was 17. I wanted an older, much more wiser man. I wanted someone who was going to make sure I was taken care of before attending to his own needs. Most importantly, I wanted someone who was going to see eye on eye with me on various levels. I found him in this one man that I'm married to. I realized early on that I didn't just find a boyfriend but I found a life mate. He was one to hold my hand, look into my eyes, and make sure that I was happy. And that's what made me fall in love with him. He let me know that he will be there for me in every way that nobody else was. This relationship was the best relationship I have ever had throughout all the ups and downs. It was always him in the beginning of my day and in the end. We stayed up talking and playing cards. I've had all kinds of late nights with my previous relationships but this was the most genuine of all. There were no bullshit or mind games here. It was just the two of us in every way, physically, mentally, emotionally, and intimately.

Relationship Trauma

In a lot of ways I did screw this relationship up. We are married and we don't have ballistic fights as we did before, however, his perception of me changed. I might be wrong, it might just be because some time has passed and relationships aren't the same after a certain point but I don't think that's all. I think that after my disorder finally came out he doesn't see me in the same light. It hurts because I know that I had a big part to do with why he doesn't look at me the same way. I have practically all of the symptoms of borderline personality disorder, which makes me a very strong case. However, there are different types of borderlines and what I am is called the "Petulant Borderline". I am always in the midst of feeling unworthy or explosively angry. Many times I have found myself unreasonably fearful, anxious, possessive, controlling, and jealous. One of my strongest characteristics that my husband is repelled by is my jealousy. It's totally understandable about why he feels this way and I don't blame him because I have realized how unreasonable and disrespectful I have been. Our fights have majorly subsided, though, and they aren't as aggressive as they used to be. However, I find myself being lost in my own mind plenty of times and that's when these fights arise.

Paranoia

My paranoia is out of hand a lot of the times. It's hard to explain how it happens but sometimes it'll hit me randomly. Sometimes I might stand in the shower and my brain picks out all the nitty-gritty details that bothered me and I'll start over analyzing them without even realizing it. I'll come to the conclusion that my husband is cheating on me in less than two minutes and my emotions rush in instantly. This paranoia is what prevents me from having any healthy relationships. This disorder is the reason why I can't live a normal connected life. This disconnection will be my demise.

As a child, I was closer with my mother since she is the one who was always there for me. She stayed up nights talking to me about everything and we would spend, every opportunity we had, together. I am a lot like her in the sense of my stubbornness and self-righteousness. She instilled this inside of me somehow and I have this quality to this day. My self-righteousness is probably the main reason for why I have no friends, not even one. I judge too quickly based on first impressions and little tidbits of a person's behavior. I end up rejecting them before I might even have a conversation with them. My excuse? They don't like me. I actually believe that this person who doesn't know me already has a negative emotion regarding me. This defense mechanism stops me from trying in order to not fail. Failure is what I fear and failure is what I always achieve in the end. Those friends that I did end up making were lost through bitter fights in which I could've judged a little less or been a little bit more passive in order to not burn down bridges. A lot of bridges were burned and that is one of my many regrets.

One of the symptoms of borderline personality disorder is identity disturbance. It's quite hard to explain what it really is without just describing the few distinct self-image perceptions I have. In certain moments I'm feeling just "okay". "Okay" feels like I look acceptable and I am going to be fine. There is no extreme supremacy or self-hatred for that matter. It's just a neutral phase. In other instances I feel confident, maybe even a little over-confident. I could act arrogant, selfish, and even superficial. I will ignore someone because they aren't as attractive as I believe they should be. This is a side of me that only developed during junior year of high school, after years of bullying, and torment that I experienced in school. This is the "bitchy" side of me. This is the side of me that I wanted to be in high school but I came out as her a little too late. If I were she earlier on, then I would've never been stomped on. The other side of me is the suicidal and self-pitying character that I battle with more often than I like to. She brings me down a lot of the times and she is my demon. The negativity she feeds off is what kills me piece by piece. These characters switch on and off periodically.

He Saved Me

Before I met my husband I was seeing a guy who was my first official, long-term boyfriend. Since he was my first I was vulnerable to his manipulations and mind games. At first I was miserable and I felt completely alone. However, after that, I started cheating. I was cheating so often that I couldn't keep track of whom I was talking to and who I had plans to meet up with. I had multiple dates every week that included a lot of unprotected sex. This impulsive behavior led me down a spiral of destructive behavior. I lost a lot of weight and I wasn't acting like myself anymore. I was short-tempered all the time, I wasn't coming home for nights at a time, and I smoking a lot of pot. As soon as I had the confidence to break up with this guy I doubled on the dates and I was seeing a different guy almost every night. They all didn't matter to me. Their names didn't matter, their lives didn't matter, and I just didn't care about them. The only guy who really mattered was my husband. He really picked me out of this path and just held my hand. His warmth was what saved me.

Don't get me wrong; maintaining a healthy relationship with my husband is one of the greatest challenges in my day-to-day life, but we work together and I know that there is hope for the long run. I find that this is the strength that I need to overcome my disease. Long with my husband, I found other ways to greatly improve my body and mind. In the next chapter, I will go over various healthy techniques that I found which help me every day to improve the way my body and mind function. Without these things, it makes it so difficult to cope with borderline personality disorder. But with a few tips and tricks, anyone can find it much more manageable to deal with daily life.

Finding Help

One of my biggest challenges still remains finding help, the help that I know I need. A very difficult part of the process is getting along with the therapist and psychiatrists. It is difficult for me to get along with people in my life, and the therapists and psychiatrists are no exception. This makes it fairly difficult to find the right help. Don't let this discourage you; just keep searching until you find someone that you can get along with. It took me dozens of therapists before I was able to find one that understood me and didn't criticize me negatively. I don't like being pushed on medication either. Because, I know I don't need medication. Doctors are so quick to put you on meds but we all know that in the long rung, it does more harm than good. I know I have my fair share of issues, but I am not psychotic, I can easily function as long as I deal with the occasional mental battles.

I refuse to be put on mind-altering medicines that will affect my brain in the long term. I'd much rather seek alternative forms of help. I have found the following to be super helpful for me and other people with Borderline. The number one most helpful thing is meditation.

Meditation quiets the mind in an almost permanent way, assuming you practice on a daily basis. It has been one of the biggest turning points in my life when I started practicing daily meditation. It helps me overcome difficult situations where before I would snap, now I simply breath through the tough moments until they pass.

Regular exercise can be life changing for anyone, especially those suffering from borderline personality disorders. There are so many health benefits to exercising regularly, I have found that it tires my body and mind; this seems to prevent my outbursts dramatically. I usually exercise for about 45 minutes in the mornings and another 30 minutes in the evening. I found this to be ideal for me. Experiment and try various different exercising techniques to see which work best for you.

Maintaining a healthy diet might be one of the key reasons why my condition has been much easier to manage lately. My diet has never been perfect by any stretch. Junk food seems to enhance the borderline personality. Cutting gunk food and fast food out of my diet dramatically improved my mental health, which ultimately eliminated my crazy behavior. Get the FREE REPORT, which details 20 super fruits and veggies that will greatly help your body and mind, that is my thank you to you for reading my book.

Conclusion

At the end of the day, I know that this disorder has affected my life in an indescribable way. Everyday is still a struggle but I try to fight it with, whether it is, keeping up a positive attitude of distracting myself with responsibilities and goals. I hope that one-day I will proudly say that I don't suffer with Borderline Personality Disorder but I know that'll take years. Hopefully, this book helped you take a brief glimpse into the messy life of a Borderline Personality.

URGENT PLEA!

Thank you for downloading my book!
I really appreciate all of your feedback, and I really like hearing what you have to say.
I need your input to make the next version better.
Please leave me a helpful REVIEW by turning this page.
Thanks so much!!
~Nikole Lev

STOP: BEFORE YOU GO
As a Thank You for reading my book,
Claim Your FREE Bonus By Clicking Below

SUPER FRUITS and VEGGIES

20 Superfoods That Will Transform Your Health

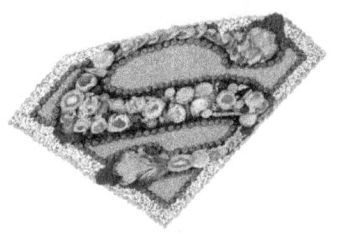

Hanna M. Krem

Just to say thank you for downloading my book, I would like to give you a 20 Super Fruits And Veggies Report 100% FREE!